SCIENCE is MAGIC

Written by
STEVE MOULD

Written by Steve Mould
Consultant Lisa Burke

Senior editor Phil Hunt
Project art editor Emma Hobson
Design assistant and illustrator Xiao Lin

Senior designer Joanne Clark
Senior editor Sam Priddy
Editorial assistant Katie Lawrence
Jacket designer Joanne Clark
Jacket co-ordinator Issy Walsh
DTP designer Mohd Rizwan
Picture researcher Sakshi Saluja
Managing editor Laura Gilbert
Managing art editor Diane Peyton Jones
Senior producer Isabell Schart
Senior producer, pre-production Nikoleta Parasaki
Creative director Helen Senior
Publishing director Sarah Larter

First published in Great Britain in 2019 by
Dorling Kindersley Limited
80 Strand, London, WC2R 0RL

A CIP catalogue record for this book
is available from the British Library.
ISBN: 978-0-2413-5826-9

Printed and bound in China.

A WORLD OF IDEAS:
SEE ALL THERE IS TO KNOW

www.dk.com

CONTENTS

IS THIS MAGIC??

WOW! IT'S FLOATING!

HOW DID THEY DO IT?

4

MEET THE AUTHOR

This book is full of experiments that explore the magic of science and the science of magic.

You'll find out how spellbinding effects like levitation, invisibility, and mind control can be re-created in your own home. And you'll learn from the greats of magic and science, from Harry Houdini to Isaac Newton.

The world is full of mysteries that seem like magic until you work them out. We'll be exploring some of those too, such as dazzling light shows in the sky, called auroras, and the peculiar rocks that sail, apparently unaided, through the California desert.

We'll also be taking a look at the supernatural. So if you want to find out about ghosts, fortune-tellers, and healing crystals then read on... the truth is stranger than fiction!

Steve Mould

HOW THE BOOK WORKS

Ready to become a science magician? Learn some amazing experiments to wow your friends, find out how magicians use science in their most famous tricks, and discover the magic of the world around you.

NOTE TO PARENTS

The activities in this book may require adult help and supervision, depending on your child's age and ability. Always ensure that your child uses tools that are appropriate for their age, and offer help and supervision as necessary to keep them safe. The Publisher cannot accept any liability for injury, loss, or damage to any property or user following suggestions in this book.

Some tricks have additional challenges.

SCIENCE TRICKS

Most of the book is made up of cool tricks, which are really science experiments. Impress your audience and then explain the science behind the magic.

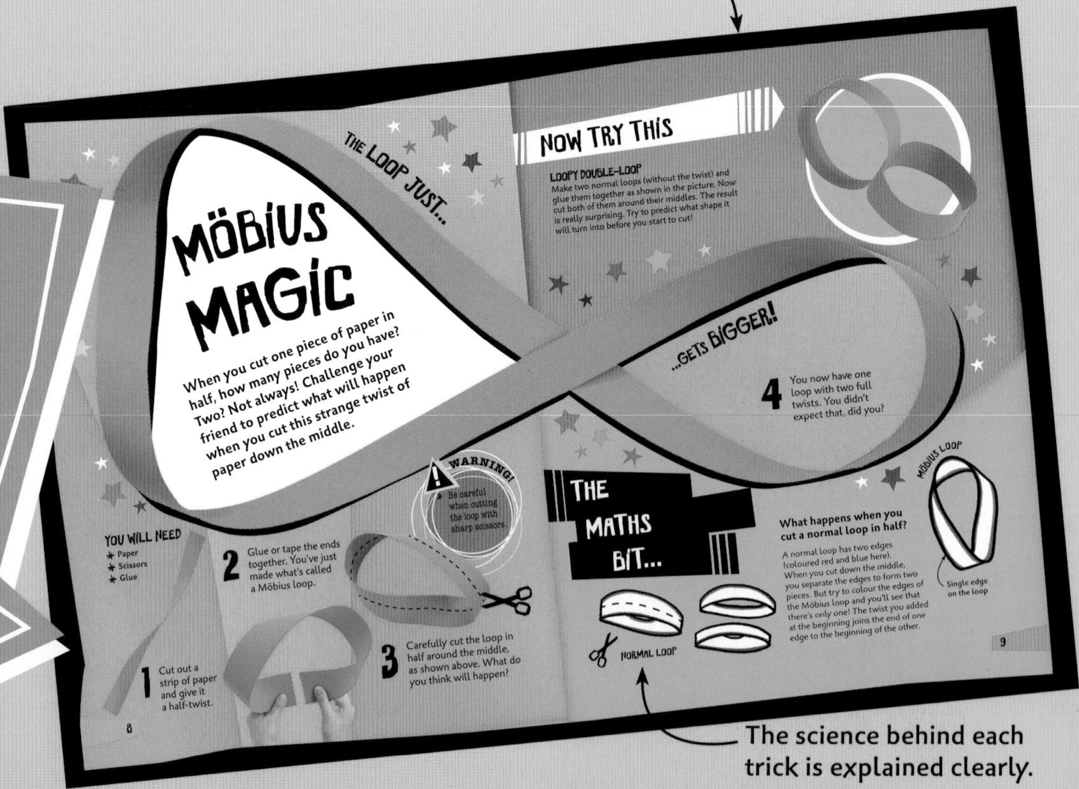

THE LOOP JUST...
MÖBIUS MAGIC
When you cut one piece of paper in half, how many pieces do you have? Two? Not always! Challenge your friend to predict what will happen when you cut this strange twist of paper down the middle.
WARNING!
Be careful when cutting the loop with sharp scissors.
YOU WILL NEED
Paper
Scissors
Glue
1 Cut out a strip of paper and give it a half-twist.
2 Glue or tape the ends together. You've just made what's called a Möbius loop.
3 Carefully cut the loop in half around the middle, as shown above. What do you think will happen?
8
NOW TRY THIS
LOOPY DOUBLE-LOOP
Make two normal loops (without the twist) and glue them together as shown in the picture. Now cut both of them around their middles. The result is really surprising. Try to predict what shape it will turn into before you start to cut!
...GETS BIGGER!
4 You now have one loop with two full twists. You didn't expect that, did you?
THE MATHS BIT...
What happens when you cut a normal loop in half?
A normal loop has two edges (coloured red and blue here). When you cut down the middle, you separate the edges to form two pieces. But try to colour the edges of the Möbius loop and you'll see that there's only one! The twist you added at the beginning joins the end of one edge to the beginning of the other.
MÖBIUS LOOP
Single edge on the loop
NORMAL LOOP
9

The science behind each trick is explained clearly.

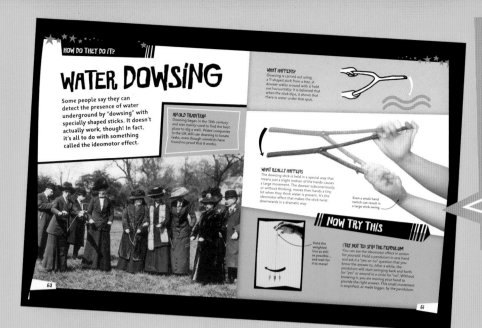

WATER DOWSING

Some people say they can detect the presence of water underground by "dowsing" with specially shaped sticks. It doesn't actually work, though! In fact, it's all to do with something called the ideomotor effect.

AN OLD TRADITION
Dowsing began in the 16th century and was mainly used to find the best place to dig a well. Water companies in the UK still use dowsing to locate leaks, even though scientists have found no proof that it works.

WHAT HAPPENS?
Dowsing is carried out using a Y-shaped stick from a tree. A dowser walks around with it held out horizontally. It is believed that when the stick dips, it shows that there is water under that spot.

WHAT REALLY HAPPENS
The dowsing stick is held in a special way that means just a slight motion of the hands causes a large movement. The dowser subconsciously, or without thinking, moves their hands a tiny bit when they think water is present. It's the ideomotor effect that makes the stick twist downwards in a dramatic way.

Even a small hand twitch can result in a large stick swing.

NOW TRY THIS

Hold the weighted line as still as possible... and wait for it to move!

(TRY NOT TO) SPIN THE PENDULUM
You can see the ideomotor effect in action for yourself. Hold a pendulum in one hand and ask it a "yes-or-no" question that you know the answer to. After a while, the pendulum will start swinging back and forth for "yes" or around in a circle for "no". Without knowing it, you are moving your hand to provide the right answer. This small movement is amplified, or made bigger, by the pendulum.

60

61

HOW DO THEY DO IT?
It turns out that some of the most famous magic tricks in history actually rely on really cool science. Find out how they did it on these pages.

SCIENCE WONDERS
It's not just tricks that seem magical – the world is full of incredible natural wonders. The most puzzling mysteries are explained in this book.

SOMETHING FISHY

If you go diving off the coast of Japan you might see these beautiful patterns on the seafloor. But what are they? Underwater crop circles? Mermaid art? Alien messages? Thanks to scientists, we now have the answer...

PUFFERFISH PATTERNS
The male white-spotted pufferfish builds his structure by swimming through the sand to form these patterned ridges. It takes about a week to complete, but it must be constantly rebuilt because of sea currents. Why does the male make this nest? To attract a mate – if a female pufferfish likes the pattern, she will lay her eggs in the middle for the male to fertilize.

SANDY STRUCTURE
These pretty undersea sand sculptures are about 2 m (6½ ft) wide, with a central area made up of much finer sand. They were first discovered in 1995, but it took scientists another 16 years to work out that they are the nests of a male fish.

16

17

Safety first!

When you see the warning symbol on an activity, it means you will need an adult to help or supervise you. Keep an eye out for these symbols throughout the book!

Take particular care when:

» Using sharp objects, such as scissors or knives.

» Using hot or boiling water.

» You are doing anything outside. It is important to always be aware of your surroundings.

» You are lifting anything heavy.

» You are lifting anything slippery.

MÖBIUS MAGIC

When you cut one piece of paper in half, how many pieces do you have? Two? Not always! Challenge your friend to predict what will happen when you cut this strange twist of paper down the middle.

YOU WILL NEED
* Paper
* Scissors
* Glue

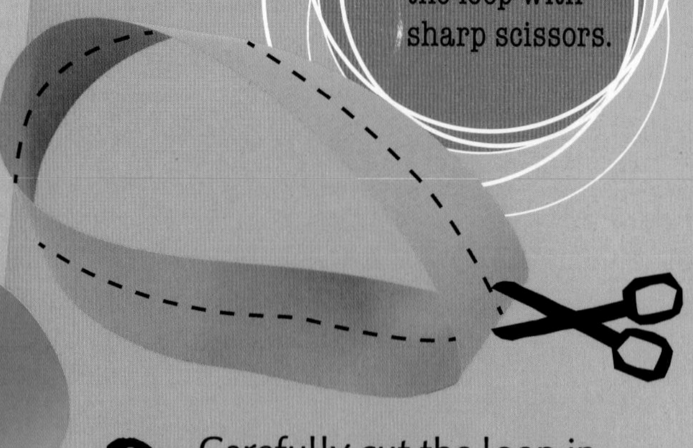

WARNING!

» Be careful when cutting the loop with sharp scissors.

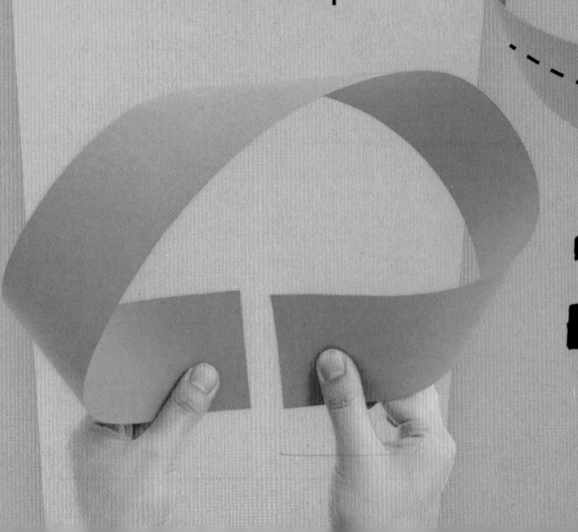

1 Cut out a strip of paper and give it a half-twist.

2 Glue or tape the ends together. You've just made what's called a Möbius loop.

3 Carefully cut the loop in half around the middle, as shown above. What do you think will happen?

NOW TRY THIS

LOOPY DOUBLE-LOOP

Make two normal loops (without the twist) and glue them together as shown in the picture. Now cut both of them around their middles. The result is really surprising. Try to predict what shape it will turn into before you start to cut!

...GETS BIGGER!

4 You now have one loop with two full twists. You didn't expect that, did you?

THE MATHS BIT...

NORMAL LOOP

What happens when you cut a normal loop in half?

A normal loop has two edges (coloured red and blue here). When you cut down the middle, you separate the edges to form two pieces. But try to colour the edges of the Möbius loop and you'll see that there's only one! The twist you added at the beginning joins the end of one edge to the beginning of the other.

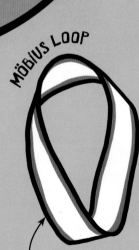

MÖBIUS LOOP

Single edge on the loop

YOU WILL NEED
* Rubber gloves
* Large Pyrex® beaker
* Vegetable oil
* Small Pyrex® tube
* Water

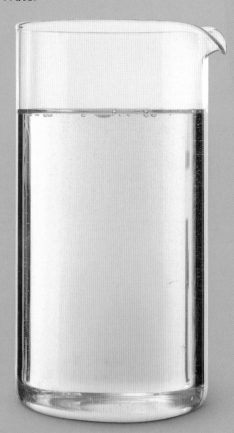

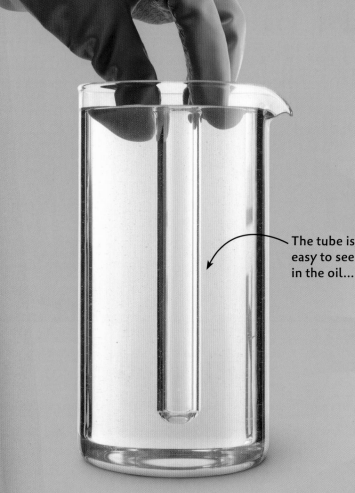

The tube is easy to see in the oil...

1 Put on some rubber gloves and fill the large beaker about three-quarters full with oil.

2 Take the small Pyrex® tube and carefully insert it into the oil.

DISAPPEARING GLASS

You've probably seen magicians make objects like coins or playing cards disappear. Here's a disappearing act you can do yourself using the science of bending light.

Try the experiment again, but this time fill the beaker halfway with water before adding the oil. The tube is now visible... but only in the water! Read The Science Bit to find out why.

...and now it's gone!

3 Now push the small tube down to allow oil to flow into it. Watch the tube disappear as the oil rises up!

The water stays at the bottom, giving you a peek at the tube inside.

THE SCIENCE BIT...

When you turn on a light, it shines on everything, bouncing off objects and into your eyes. Glass, though, is transparent, meaning that light passes *through it* instead of bouncing off it.

If light doesn't bounce off glass into your eyes, how can you see it? It's because light bends a bit when it passes from air to glass. If you look at a glass, the light coming through from behind it bends and everything looks wobbly (*see image, right*). When light passes from oil to glass, it hardly bends – dipping the glass in oil, the wobbles go away and the glass disappears! Light bends a bit between water and glass, which is why you can see the glass in water.

THE FLOATING BALLOON

YOU WILL NEED
* Two dry erase marker pens (preferably new)
* Dinner plate
* Jug of water

1 Draw a nice, thick balloon on a plate with dry erase markers.

The balloon will start to lift away from the plate.

2 Slowly pour water onto the plate until the balloon is covered.

THE SCIENCE BIT...

WHITEBOARD AND WIPER

The ink inside most pens is sticky, but not in a dry erase marker pen.

With a normal pen, you don't want your writing to get rubbed off or smudged. With dry erase markers, you can wipe the ink off easily. These pens have a special chemical in them that forms a slippery layer between the ink and the writing surface. Once the ink has dried, it can be lifted off in one piece.

Imagine if you could draw a picture and cast a spell to make it come to life! We'll show you how with a few simple ingredients.

3 Watch as the balloon peels off the plate and floats on the surface of the water. If any of the balloon remains stuck on the plate, you can blow on it to bring it to life!

FLOATING LIKE A CORK
For this trick to work, the ink needs to float. Luckily, just like a cork, the ink in a dry erase marker is less dense, or lighter, than water so will rise to the surface.

THE INK DOES NOT BREAK UP IN WATER, SO STAYS IN ONE PIECE.

HOUDINI'S WATER ESCAPE

The "Chinese Water Torture Cell" was a trick made famous by the great Harry Houdini in the early 1900s. He was able to hold his breath for long enough to escape from a locked tank of water.

Name:
HARRY HOUDINI

Date of Birth:
24 March 1874

Profession:
Escapologist

Signature: *Harry Houdini*

Hungarian-born Ehrich Weisz moved to the United States in 1876 and later took the stage name of Harry Houdini. One of the world's greatest escapologists, he was famous for being able to escape from padlocks, chains, and even coffins!

THE STUNT

Houdini was lowered upside down into a specially built water tank with his feet shackled to the top. Audience members were allowed to check that the tank was sealed and the locks were secure. Then everything was hidden under a cover. Suspense built over the next 3 minutes before Houdini emerged to wild applause. Houdini was a master at picking locks, which might explain how he could release his feet. It may also be true that the shackles had a secret release mechanism. The big mystery is how he was able to survive underwater for so long.

HOLDING YOUR BREATH – WHAT HAPPENS?

The key to Houdini's impressive trick was his ability to hold his breath for a *really* long time. Breathing air into your lungs is how your body gets oxygen into your blood, where it's used to make energy. In the process, it's converted into carbon dioxide, which you breathe out. When you hold your breath (**which can be dangerous, so don't try this yourself!**), the carbon dioxide builds up in your body and increases the levels of acid in your blood. Here's how Houdini fought the body's basic need to breathe:

1. Through practice, he was able to slow his body down and use up oxygen more slowly. His heart rate would decrease and his body would only send blood to vital organs such as his brain.

2. Houdini increased his lung capacity by keeping fit and performing on an empty stomach. This meant he could breathe in more air.

3. He used meditation to reduce the urge to breathe.

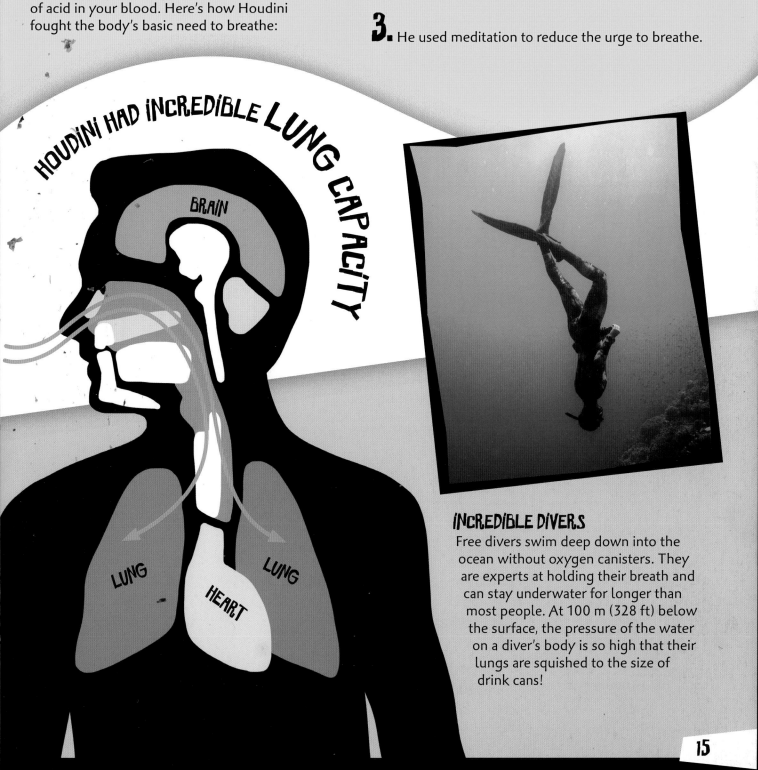

HOUDINI HAD INCREDIBLE LUNG CAPACITY

BRAIN

LUNG

LUNG

HEART

INCREDIBLE DIVERS

Free divers swim deep down into the ocean without oxygen canisters. They are experts at holding their breath and can stay underwater for longer than most people. At 100 m (328 ft) below the surface, the pressure of the water on a diver's body is so high that their lungs are squished to the size of drink cans!

15

SCIENCE WONDERS

SOMETHING FISHY

If you go diving off the coast of Japan you might see these beautiful patterns on the seafloor. But what are they? Underwater crop circles? Mermaid art? Alien messages? Thanks to scientists, we now have the answer...

SANDY STRUCTURE

These pretty undersea sand sculptures are about 2 m (6½ ft) wide, with a central area made up of much finer sand. They were first discovered in 1995, but it took scientists another 16 years to work out that they are the nests of a male fish.

PUFFERFISH PATTERNS

The male white-spotted pufferfish builds his structure by swimming through the sand to form these patterned ridges. It takes about a week to complete, but it must be constantly rebuilt because of sea currents. Why does the male make this nest? To attract a mate — if a female pufferfish likes the pattern, she will lay her eggs in the middle for the male to fertilize.

MAGNETIC FINGERS

In this trick you'll convince your friends you can move their fingers with just the power of your mind!

1 Ask your friend to clasp their hands, pushing them together with a light pressure on the palms. Now tell them you are going to make their fingers become magnetic.

2 Next, ask your friend to raise their two index fingers and hold them apart.

i AM CONTROLLING YOUR MIND!

18

3 This is where your magical talking skills come in. Tell your friend you are controlling their fingers with your mind and that they won't be able to resist them coming together. As you talk, you will see that their fingers start to move towards each other. Tell them to fight against it, but they won't be able to – it actually makes it worse!

BENDING YOUR FINGERS ACTUALLY USES MUSCLES IN YOUR ARM, NOT YOUR HAND.

THE SCIENCE BIT...

Everything is linked...

Your friend feels as if their fingers are being pulled together because of the position of their hands. The muscles you use to extend a finger are linked to all the other fingers on that hand. With your other fingers bent, the muscles holding up your index fingers will get tired quickly. Trying to hold the two index fingers apart will make the muscles even more tired. The tired muscles can't support the outstretched index fingers, so they move closer and closer together.

HAND MUSCLES

NOW TRY THIS

Bend your middle finger and put your hand on a table, palm facing down. You will be able to lift your thumb, index, and little finger, but you will find it impossible to lift your ring finger.

Ring finger

WHAT'S HAPPENING?
The tissue that connects a muscle to a bone is called a tendon. Fingers have separate tendons, except for the middle and ring fingers, which share one – when your middle finger is bent, your ring finger feels stuck.

BEND THE FAN BLADES

Spinning fan blades look really strange when you see them through a smartphone camera...

YOU WILL NEED

* Hand-held fan
* Smartphone

The blades will seem to twist and bend.

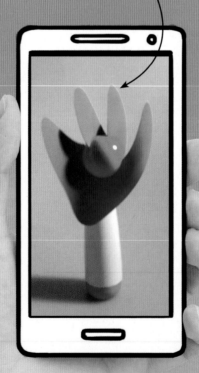

1

Go outside on a bright, sunny day and turn on a hand-held fan. Look at it through a smartphone camera... something very strange will happen!

THIS IS CALLED THE ROLLING SHUTTER EFFECT.

THE SCIENCE BIT...

Digital cameras like the one in a smartphone have something inside them called a sensor, which captures the image.

The sensor is an electronic device made of millions of smaller sensors called pixels. Each one records a different tiny piece of the picture. However, when you take a picture, these pixels don't all work at the same time to build the image. Instead, they start at the top and quickly work down to the bottom. This means that the bottom of a digital picture captures a moment slightly later in time than the top. So if something is moving fast, like a fan blade or skateboarder, it will appear distorted.

REAL TIME   DIGITAL IMAGE

Red line shows sensors working from top to bottom to build up the image.

In this final picture the skateboarder has moved further along at the bottom of the image than at the top.

NOW TRY THIS

SPINNER
Other objects that turn quickly also work. Try looking at a spinning fidget spinner.

FIDGET SPINNER

Sometimes the arms look like they're shrinking...

...and other times like they're growing!

YOU WILL NEED
* Mug
* Empty drink can

Make sure the can is empty.

1 Place the can inside the mug. Make sure the mug is big enough to leave a little gap around the sides.

2 Blow down hard into the gap between the can and the mug – the can will shoot out! Blow slightly from the side so you don't get hit.

JUMPING DRINK CAN

Challenge a friend to remove an empty drink can from a mug without touching the can or turning the mug upside down. They'll find it tricky! The secret? It's all to do with the science of air pressure.

THE SCIENCE BIT...

When you blow into the gap between the can and the mug, the force of the air squeezes the air that's already down there.

When you try to squeeze air like this, the air pushes back in all directions. In other words, you're making the air pressure increase. This high-pressure air then pushes against the bottom of the can, which results in it rising up and flying out of the mug.

The can rises up out of the mug.

Air is blown into the side of the mug.

Air pressure increases.

23

YOU WILL NEED

* Bottle
* Banknote
* Three coins the same size – they should be larger than the hole in the top of the bottle

The banknote should be sticking out a bit more on one side.

1

Arrange the banknote and coins as shown. Challenge your friend to remove the banknote without the coins falling off. They can only touch the note, not the coins.

2

They won't be able to do it... and the coins will go everywhere! Now it's your turn. First, secretly lick your index finger or wet it under a tap.

THE SALIVA MAKES YOUR FINGER STICKY!

MONEY GRABBER

Here's a chance to beat your friend in a banknote challenge. All it takes is a speedy finger and a little science know-how about moving objects.

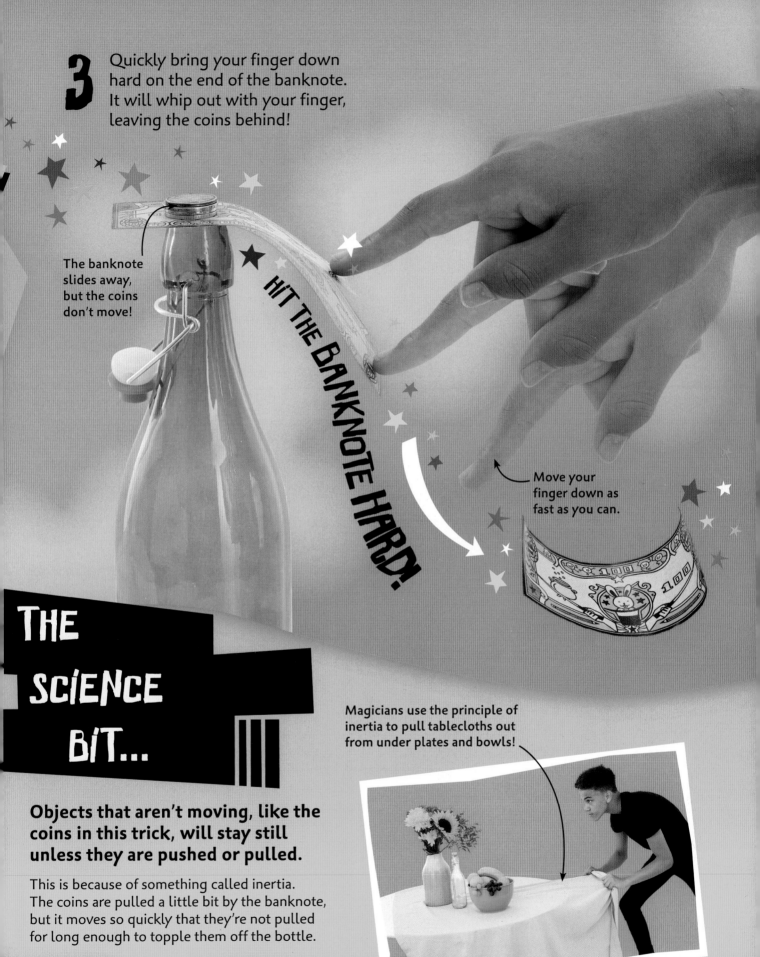

3 Quickly bring your finger down hard on the end of the banknote. It will whip out with your finger, leaving the coins behind!

The banknote slides away, but the coins don't move!

HIT THE BANKNOTE HARD!

Move your finger down as fast as you can.

THE SCIENCE BIT...

Magicians use the principle of inertia to pull tablecloths out from under plates and bowls!

Objects that aren't moving, like the coins in this trick, will stay still unless they are pushed or pulled.

This is because of something called inertia. The coins are pulled a little bit by the banknote, but it moves so quickly that they're not pulled for long enough to topple them off the bottle.

READING MINDS

Psychics and fortune-tellers have been in the mind-reading business for hundreds of years. Using props like picture cards called tarot cards, and horoscopes, they even claim to read the future! Here are some of their techniques...

PSYCHIC TRICKERY

Fortune-tellers use different ways to make you think they have special powers. They might read your palm, stare into a crystal ball, or tell you about yourself using tarot cards. While people want to believe that what they are being told is true, a fortune-teller's real skill is being able to talk very generally and make the most of any reaction from the person they are "reading".

TAROT CARDS

MAKING IT PERSONAL

If fortune-tellers don't know anything about someone in advance, it's called "cold reading". A trick they use in this situation is to say things that apply to almost everyone but that feel really personal. For example, "You like being with friends but sometimes like to be on your own" or "You don't like other people telling you what to think". Horoscopes use this technique, too.

"YOU WILL RECEIVE SOME MONEY."

Horoscopes are split into 12 signs, which are based on the time of year you were born.

CONFIRMATION BIAS

A fortune-teller will make many statements about you during a reading. Some of them will be completely wrong! But because of something called confirmation bias, you will only remember the things they got right!

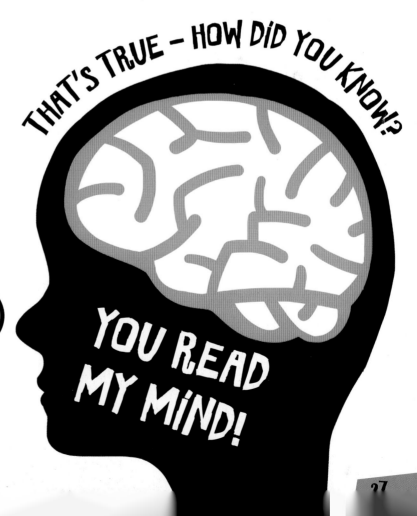

You like playing football (true). You have a pet dog (false). You love eating ice cream (true).

That mind reader was amaaaazing!

Why?

She knew I liked playing football and eating ice cream.

Wow!

THAT'S TRUE — HOW DID YOU KNOW?

YOU READ MY MIND!

THE NORTHERN LIGHTS
This spectacular picture of the aurora borealis was taken in the Lofoten Islands in north Norway. The chances of seeing an aurora here depend on the strength of the solar wind. When it's really strong, you might see other colours such as scarlet and orange.

COSMIC AURORAS

If you travel to countries near the North and South poles, you might see a sensational light show in the sky. Both the aurora borealis in the north and the aurora australis in the south look like huge, wavy curtains of colour, created by particles from the Sun entering Earth's atmosphere.

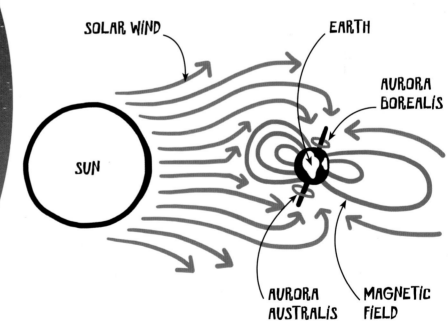

SOLAR WIND

EARTH

AURORA BOREALIS

SUN

AURORA AUSTRALIS

MAGNETIC FIELD

CREATED BY THE SUN

As well as light, the Sun sends out tiny particles called electrons, which are carried to Earth on a super-fast solar wind. As Earth is like a giant magnet, the electrons are pulled to the poles by the magnetic field. When they hit tiny oxygen particles in our atmosphere, the oxygen glows green in the sky.

YOU WILL NEED
* TV
* TV remote control
* Small hand-held mirror
* Smartphone (optional)

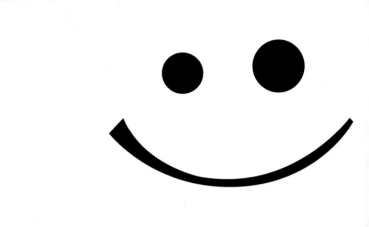

1 Try to turn on the TV with the remote control pointing in the wrong direction. It will be impossible.

INVISIBLE LIGHT BEAMS

A TV remote control can seem like a magic wand if you don't know how it works. This fun challenge shows how it's all to do with invisible light called infrared.

2 Put a small mirror in front of the remote. You need to angle it so the invisible beams from the remote reflect off the mirror towards the TV. This might take a bit of practice! When you get it right, the TV will come on. Now challenge a friend to try to do it without revealing the secret of the mirror. When they can't, show them how it's done!

IT REFLECTS!

When you press a remote control, nothing lights up at the end of the remote. However, if you press a button on the remote while looking at it through a smartphone camera, you'll see a small flashing light on the phone screen. Humans can't see infrared light *(see below)*, but the camera in a smartphone is able to pick it up.

THE SCIENCE BIT...

Light is made up of a spectrum, or range, of colours...

We can only see a part of the spectrum, between blue and red. Beyond red is infrared light. Your remote control sends bursts of this light to the TV. The pattern of bursts tells the TV what to do.

LIGHT SPECTRUM

Infrared light cannot be seen by the human eye.

Infrared light can be used to detect heat. Some snakes have organs to sense this light, which helps them find prey.

HUMAN VISION

SNAKE VISION

Your friend won't notice you're pushing away from their body, they'll just think you're pushing downwards.

1

Ask your friend to stand on one leg and hold their arms out. Push down on one arm and tell them to try to stop you moving it. Secretly push a little bit away from their body – this will cause them to stumble.

THE POWER OF A MAGIC CRYSTAL

Some scammers will use sneaky science to try to trick you out of your money. They will tell you they have crystals that will give you super balance or good health. But they don't actually work! Here's one way they fool people into believing them.

This time, you're pushing slightly towards your friend's body, but again they will think you're pushing downwards.

2

Repeat the test, this time giving your friend the crystal to hold. Tell them it will give them extra strength and balance. Now push down and slightly towards their body – they will be able to resist no matter how hard you push!

THE SCIENCE BIT...

This is nothing to do with the crystal, but everything to do with balance.

In the first test, you push slightly away from your friend's feet. This forces them off balance. In the second test, you push towards their feet so their balance isn't affected.

As well as using fake balance tests, scammers make the most of something called the placebo effect. They will give a sick person fake "healing crystals" or pills that don't work, but the sick person starts to feel better anyway. That's because simply believing a treatment works makes people feel better – the placebo effect!

1 Very carefully chop half a red cabbage into small pieces.

COLOUR-CHANGING POTION

If you thought cabbages were boring, think again. In this trick you will make an incredible colour-changing cabbage potion.

2 Ask an adult to pour boiling water into a jug. Carefully add the chopped cabbage. Leave it to cool for 10 minutes.

3 Pour the cabbage water through a sieve into another jug. Now add cold water until the liquid is purple but still see-through.

YOU WILL NEED

* Half a red cabbage
* Knife
* Chopping board
* Boiling water
* Two jugs
* Sieve
* Three glasses
* Teaspoon
* White vinegar
* Bicarbonate of soda

4 It's time to stun your audience. In front of your friends, pour your potion into three glasses. With a magical flourish add some white vinegar to one glass, drop by drop. It changes colour! Now mix a teaspoon of bicarbonate of soda into another glass. Watch your friends' jaws drop as it turns a completely different colour.

THE SCIENCE BIT...

The trick works because of the amount of acid in the liquid.

Acidity is measured using something called the pH scale. Strong acids have a pH of around 1, while strong bases – the opposites of acids – have a pH of around 14. Cabbage juice contains something called anthocyanin, which changes colour if something is an acid or a base. Acids such as vinegar turn the cabbage juice pink, while bases such as bicarbonate of soda turn it blue or green.

PH SCALE

CHOCOLATE

TOOTHPASTE

0 1 2 3 4 5 6 7 8 9 10 11 12 13 14

LEMON

PEANUTS

WATER

SOAPY WATER

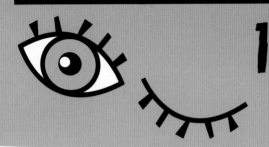

1 Close your right eye. Hold this image of a dot and a cross about 30 cm (12 in) from your face. Look at the cross. You will also see the dot in the corner of your vision.

2 Slowly move the page closer to your face. The dot will suddenly disappear.

DISAPPEARING

THE SCIENCE BIT...

This is all about your blind spot, a point in your eye where you literally cannot see.

When light enters your eyes, it hits a thin layer at the back called the retina. This contains special cells called photoreceptors that convert the light into electrical signals. These are sent to your brain, where they are processed into images. The electric signals travel along tiny, wire-like nerves that come together in a bundle called the optic nerve. As there's no space for photoreceptors at the head of this nerve, you're blind in that spot. Our clever brains fill in the gap at this point based on what it sees around it, which in the case of our tricks are the white and green backgrounds.

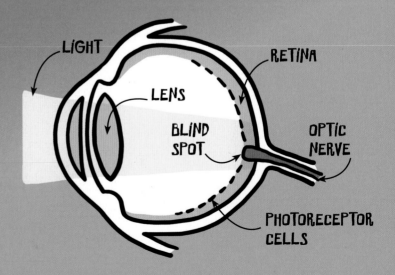

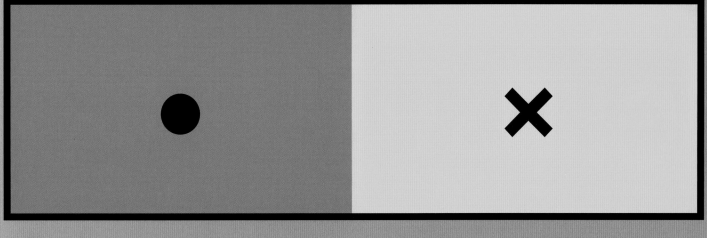

3 It even works with colours. Do the same thing with this coloured box. This time, when you reach the blind spot the black dot will appear to turn green.

WHERE HAS THE DOT GONE?!

DOTS

Magic tricks often rely on fooling your senses. In this experiment, you'll see how to trick your own eyes using the science of sight.

NOW TRY THIS

As your eyes move around the page you might notice something moving down here in the corner...

This is a motion illusion – something still that looks like it's moving. The swirly lines only seem to move when your eyes move. No one really knows why this happens, but it has something to do with how our brain processes this combination of colours and shades. It will really be swirling as you read this!

GHOSTLY VISIONS

Ghosts aren't real. However, some magicians will add ghoulish illusions to their show for a spooky twist. Here's how they do it...

SCARING THE CROWD

In London during the late 19th century, people would pay to watch shows where ghosts seemed to appear on stage. Today, you can see the same illusions in theme parks around the world, on rides such as the ghost train.

SEEING THE GHOST WOULD MAKE YOU SCREAM!

Mirrored glass redirects ghost image to the stage and also enables audience to see it through the glass.

WOW!

"Ghost" on the stage

Mirror reflects ghost image upwards.

Light projected onto an actor under the stage.

Actor pretending to be a ghost.

HOW DID IT WORK?
Windows are made of glass because glass is see-through. However, glass is also a bit like a mirror – it reflects things. By arranging the light, glass, and mirrors in a certain way, the audience sees a reflection of an actor under the stage.

NOW TRY THIS

SEE YOURSELF AS A "GHOST"
When you look out of the window during the day, you can see what's outside, but at night you only see your reflection. You don't see your reflection in the day because it's much fainter than the light outside. However, at a certain time between day and night – around dusk – you'll see your reflection *and* what's outside mixed together. You will look like a ghost!

ROCKY MYSTERY

These mysterious rocks with long tracks have moved across the desert. But how? Known as "sailing stones", they puzzled scientists for many years until the truth was finally uncovered...

DEATH VALLEY STONES

"Sailing stones" are found in parts of the desert where the ground is very smooth and flat, like Death Valley in California, USA. Here, puzzled scientists eventually solved the mystery by attaching devices to the rocks to track their position. They also set up time-lapse cameras that showed the rocks moving across the sand.

SOLVING THE PUZZLE

Scientists found that shallow ponds sometimes formed on the desert floor and froze at night. As the ice began to melt in the sun, it broke into large sheets that floated on the water. When the wind blew, the ice – and the rocks trapped inside it – moved across the slippery mud.

WIND

ICE

ROCK

WATER

MUD

1

Tie at least 10 strands of tinsel together at one end with a single knot. Tie another knot about 10 cm (4 in) down from the first knot and use scissors to cut off any extra tinsel at the ends.

The strands are very thin, so you will have to really concentrate when tying the knot.

2

Use the microfibre cloth to rub up and down the PVC pipe for about 30 seconds. Rub hard until you can hear the pipe start to crackle.

YOU WILL NEED

✳ Thin strands of silver Mylar® tinsel (called icicle tinsel or angel hair tinsel)
✳ Scissors
✳ PVC pipe
✳ Microfibre cloth

HOVERING TINSEL

A floating silver ball might sound like the stuff of science fiction, but this trick relies on pure science fact.

THE SCIENCE BIT...

Tiny particles called electrons on both the pipe and tinsel are repelling – or pushing away from – each other.

At the start of the trick, electrons on the cloth are passed onto the pipe when you rub it. When the tinsel touches the pipe, some of these electrons jump onto the tinsel. Because electrons repel each other, the tinsel pushes away from the pipe, while the electrons in the individual strands also repel against each other to turn the tinsel into a ball.

Electrons jump from the pipe to the tinsel.

Hold the cloth around the pipe.

3

Drop the tinsel onto the pipe, releasing it before it touches the pipe. It may take a few goes, but it will eventually pop into a ball and float above the pipe. Keep moving the pipe under the tinsel so the ball stays in the air.

1

Pour some water onto a dinner plate until it's nearly at the top of the rim.

2

Grind some black pepper onto the water so it's evenly spread.

PEPPER-REPELLING FINGER

If you always wanted magic powers at your fingertips, this is the trick for you. Knowing the secret of stretchy water enables you to repel, or push away, pepper at will...

THE SCIENCE BIT...

Water has a property called surface tension that makes the top layer stretchy like a balloon.

Washing-up liquid reduces the surface tension, so putting a soapy finger in water is like popping a balloon with a pin – the stretchy surface pulls back, carrying the pepper with it.

POPPING A BALLOON

4 Secretly put some washing-up liquid on the tip of your finger. Dip your finger into the water and watch the pepper zoom away!

3 Tell your friend to put their finger in the water. Nothing happens... because they don't have your magic powers.

LOOK AT THAT PEPPER GO!

1 Take the pack of cards and turn over the bottom card in the deck. Now, no matter which way up the deck is, the cards will look like they're facing down.

2 Fan out the cards in your hands and ask your friend to pick one. Tell them to look at it, without showing it to you.

Make sure they don't see the bottom card.

MISDIRECTION

To help bamboozle their audiences, magicians often use a technique called misdirection. This card trick shows you how to put this powerful method to work.

5 You need to turn the deck back over without your friend noticing. To do this, ask them to think of a magic word... then be sure to catch their eye as you flip the deck.

HMMM... ABRACADABRA!

3 Say your friend's name and ask them to concentrate on memorizing their card. This will make them look at you, and their focus will be directed away from the deck. You can now flip the cards over without them noticing.

Don't look down as you flip the cards.

4 Ask your friend to slot their card back into the deck anywhere they like.

Be careful they don't notice that the cards below the top card are the wrong way up.

THE SCIENCE BIT...

Quite simply, humans are not very good at doing two things at the same time.

So here, by asking your friend to remember the card or to think of a word, you are misdirecting their attention away from what you are doing – flipping the deck.

6 Fan out the cards again. Look! One card is facing up. Your friend will be amazed to discover it's their card.

SPOOKY DRINK CAN

All you need for this impressive balancing act is a can of drink and some water. With these simple items you will appear to defy the laws of gravity, the force that pulls us towards the ground...

YOU WILL NEED
* Can of drink
* Measuring jug
* Water

2 Pour about 150 ml (5 fl oz) of water into a measuring jug, then pour it into the can.

1 Drink all the liquid in your can – it needs to be completely empty.

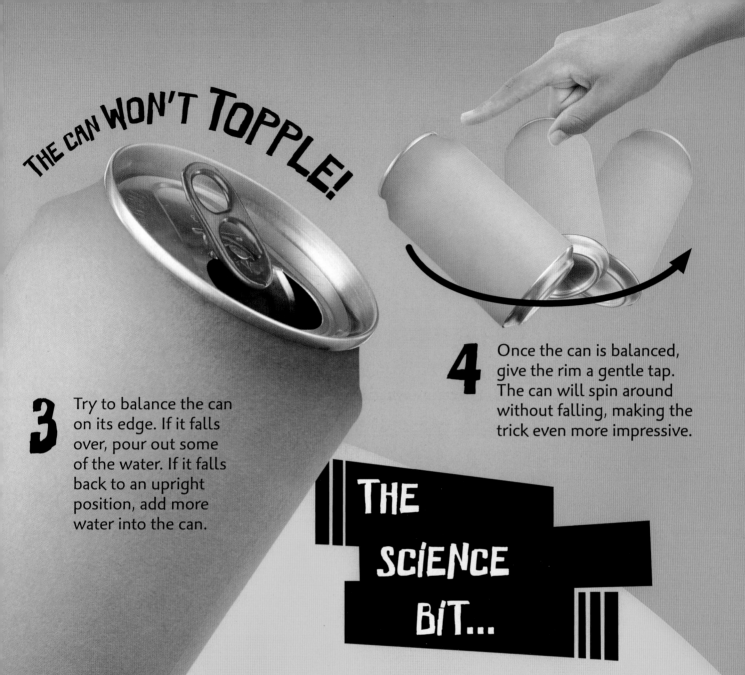

THE CAN WON'T TOPPLE!

3 Try to balance the can on its edge. If it falls over, pour out some of the water. If it falls back to an upright position, add more water into the can.

4 Once the can is balanced, give the rim a gentle tap. The can will spin around without falling, making the trick even more impressive.

THE SCIENCE BIT...

This trick works because of something called the centre of mass.

This is the central point of an object's total weight, and where it is perfectly balanced. By changing the amount of water in the can, you move the centre of mass until it's at the exact place where the can will balance.

When the can is full and tilted on its edge, the centre of mass is roughly in the middle of the can and not above the edge, so it topples over.

When you take some of the water out of the can, the centre of mass shifts across because the weight inside has moved. If you can get the centre of mass above the edge of the can, it will balance.

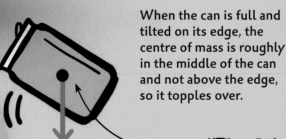

CENTRE OF MASS

INEXHAUSTIBLE BOTTLE

In this classic feat a magician pours a glass of orange juice. From the same bottle, a glass of milk is poured... then a glass of water... and a glass of wine! How? It's down to one very special bottle.

HISTORIC TRICK
This trick dates back to the 17th century and has a few different names, such as Satan's Barman, the Think-a-Drink, and Any Drink Called For. You can still buy these unique bottles in magic shops today.

With the hole uncovered, air can now get in.

The air replaces the liquid...

The magician covers the holes to stop air getting in.

The finger is raised.

Surface tension stops the liquid from escaping.

... and the liquid pours out!

SECRETS OF THE BOTTLE

This trick works because of secret finger holes on the side of the bottle. Inside are separate containers with very thin spouts leading up to the neck. For liquid to pour out of a container, air must be able to get in to replace it. Air can't get in through the spout because the tiny particles that make up liquid stick to each other and to the container's walls. This is called surface tension and it creates a barrier that stops air getting in through the tiny spout. However, each container has a separate tube leading to the holes on the outside of the bottle. This lets air in so the liquid can pour out. The magician can choose which drink appears by choosing which holes to uncover.

MILK

CRANBERRY JUICE

ORANGE JUICE

SWITCHING COLOUR

Animals that can change colour are the closest thing to magic you will find in nature. These amazing creatures copy the colours around them for camouflage, or disguise, which helps them hide from predators or sneak up on prey.

IS IT A LEAF?

This remarkable chameleon from Madagascar is brilliant at looking like... a dead leaf! It can alter its colour to perfectly match the changing shades of the forest floor and disguise itself from anything that may want to eat it.

BOTH EYES OF A PEACOCK FLOUNDER ARE ON **ONE SIDE** OF ITS HEAD.

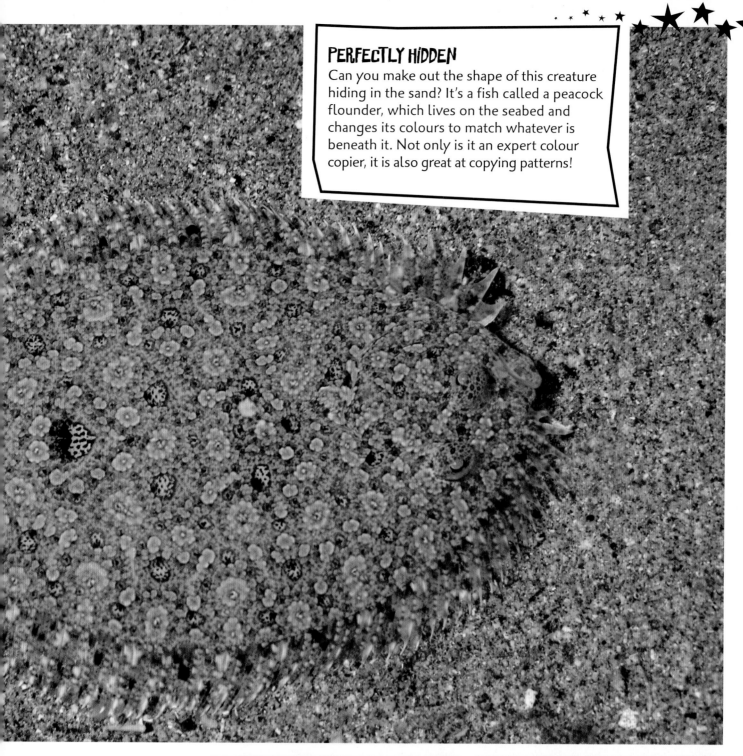

PERFECTLY HIDDEN
Can you make out the shape of this creature hiding in the sand? It's a fish called a peacock flounder, which lives on the seabed and changes its colours to match whatever is beneath it. Not only is it an expert colour copier, it is also great at copying patterns!

ALL ABOUT THE CELLS
Colour-changing animals have special cells on their skin called chromatophores. When activated, these tiny dots stretch out to transform the colour and pattern of creatures such as the cuttlefish.

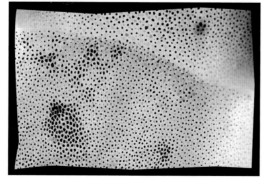

CUTTLEFISH CHROMATOPHORES (NORMAL)

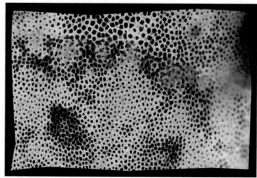

CUTTLEFISH CHROMATOPHORES (ACTIVATED)

HiDDEN PiCTURES

All is not what it seems on this page. In the mysterious picture below you will find a hidden image. To discover what it is, you will have to teach your brain to look *through* the page.

1 Hold this picture up in front of you. Try to relax your eyes so that they are looking at something beyond the page. These two dots might help...

Looking at the dots, move the page closer to your face. You will start to see double. When the dots overlap, let them "lock together". Now move the page away and look at the picture.

NOW TRY THIS

You can also use the dots trick on this one.

THE GLASS METHOD

You can try another technique on this image. Place the picture behind some flat glass. Look at your reflection in the glass, then try to focus back on the picture without moving your eyes. All will be revealed!

Turn to page 96 to find out what images are hiding on these pages.

THE SCIENCE BIT...

This is all about how your brain calculates distances.

When you look at something close up, you cross your eyes more than when you look at a faraway object. Your brain uses this to work out distances, but these pictures use a special pattern to play a trick. When you look *through* the image, your eyes become less crossed and you see double. The pattern then overlaps with itself and everything looks normal again, just a little further away. Some parts of the picture have been slightly adjusted so your eyes are more or less crossed. It's here that the "hidden" image becomes visible.

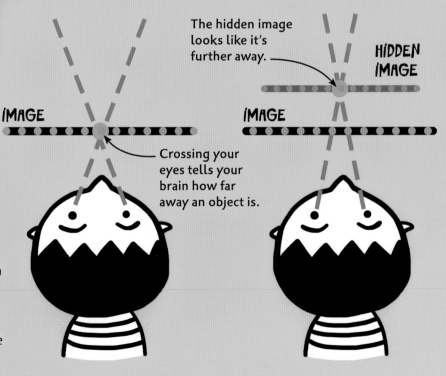

The hidden image looks like it's further away.

HIDDEN IMAGE

IMAGE

IMAGE

Crossing your eyes tells your brain how far away an object is.

YOU WILL NEED
* Pencil or pen
* Tracing paper or thin paper

WHICH CURVE is LONGER?

1 First make your prediction. Do you think the top curve is the longer of the two? Or is the bottom one longer?

CURIOUS CURVES

Here's a simple but mysterious visual trick that scientists can't explain. Can you work out which of the two curves above is longer?

2 Use tracing paper to draw around the top curve on this page.

3 Line your curve up with the bottom one. Which is longer? How strange – even though the bottom one looked longer, you've just discovered that they're both the same length!

THE SCIENCE BIT...

This visual trick is known as the "Jastrow illusion".

Scientists don't really know why the bottom curve looks longer. They think it might be because your brain compares the short inner curve of the top shape with the long outer curve of the bottom shape as they are next to each other. You see a similar illusion with these photos of the Leaning Tower of Pisa. Which tower is leaning more? It looks like the one on the right... but the images are identical!

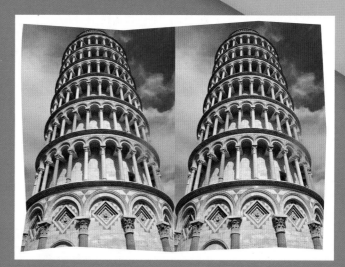

57

NO-LEAK BAG

You have probably seen the famous magic trick where an assistant is poked with swords without being harmed. Here's a similar amazing feat using a plastic bag and some pencils.

YOU WILL NEED
* Zip-lock plastic bag
* Water
* Sharp pencils

1 Fill the bag two-thirds full with water and zip it up.

2 Hold the bag firmly in one hand. Use your other hand to push a sharp pencil through the bag, into the water, and out the other side. If it's easier, have an assistant hold the bag for you – but be careful not to poke them!

The pencil goes through the bag... and no water leaks!

3

Keep adding more pencils. The bag will never leak!

THE SCIENCE BIT...

The bag doesn't leak because plastic is stretchy. Let's compare pencils going through a sheet of paper and a plastic bag...

PAPER

When you poke a pencil through paper, it rips, and gaps form around the pencil. If this was a paper bag full of water, the water would leak out through these gaps.

PLASTIC

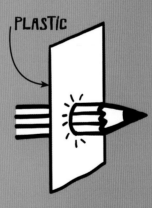

Instead of ripping, plastic stretches and moves to make room for the pencil. This creates a tight seal so the water can't leak out.

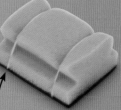

When you stretch an elastic band, it tightens against what's underneath it. This is what the plastic does around the pencil.

Plastic is stretchy like an elastic band – when it wraps around something, it squishes it.

59

WATER DOWSING

Some people say they can detect the presence of water underground by "dowsing" with specially shaped sticks. It doesn't actually work, though! In fact, it's all to do with something called the ideomotor effect.

AN OLD TRADITION

Dowsing began in the 16th century and was mainly used to find the best place to dig a well. Water companies in the UK still use dowsing to locate leaks, even though scientists have found no proof that it works.

WHAT HAPPENS?

Dowsing is carried out using a Y-shaped stick from a tree. A dowser walks around with it held out horizontally. It is believed that when the stick dips, it shows that there is water under that spot.

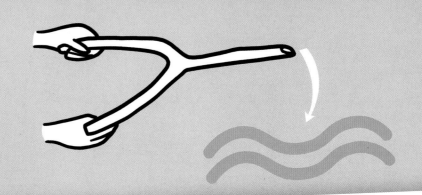

WHAT REALLY HAPPENS

The dowsing stick is held in a special way that means just a slight motion of the hands causes a large movement. The dowser subconsciously, or without thinking, moves their hands a tiny bit when they think water is present. It's the ideomotor effect that makes the stick twist downwards in a dramatic way.

Even a small hand twitch can result in a large stick swing.

NOW TRY THIS

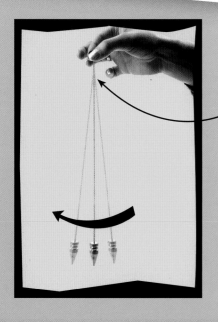

Hold the weighted line as still as possible... and wait for it to move!

(TRY NOT TO) SPIN THE PENDULUM

You can see the ideomotor effect in action for yourself. Hold a pendulum in one hand and ask it a "yes-or-no" question that you know the answer to. After a while, the pendulum will start swinging back and forth for "yes" or around in a circle for "no". Without knowing it, you are moving your hand to provide the right answer. This small movement is amplified, or made bigger, by the pendulum.

GUESS THE COIN

? **?** **?**

Become a mind reader in this simple but effective trick that will fool your friends every time. It's all about the science of heat and what happens when you hold a coin.

YOU WILL NEED
* Coins
* Blindfold

I THINK IT'S... THIS ONE!

1 Ask a friend to put a handful of coins on a table. Put on a blindfold and ask them to pick up a coin, holding it tight in their hand to add extra magic power. This is the coin you will magically select later.

Tell your friend to really focus on the coin they have chosen.

2 Ask your friend to put the coin back on the table. Remove your blindfold and say that you will find their chosen coin. Pick up each coin one by one. Pretend to be using psychic powers when what you're really doing is feeling for the warm one.

3 Ta-daaa! When you reveal the chosen coin, your friend will be amazed.

I CAN'T BELIEVE IT!

THE SCIENCE BIT...

The warm jiggling atoms in your friend's hand knock into the atoms in the metal causing them to jiggle too, making them warm. These warm metal atoms knock into other atoms and particles in the metal, causing them to jiggle, and that's how heat spreads throughout the coin.

A coin heats up in your friend's hand because of something called conduction.

If you could look through a microscope at the tiny particles called atoms in the metal, you would see that the hot ones are jiggling around a lot while the cold ones are only jiggling a little. Heat is just the jiggling of atoms, and conduction is a way for heat to move through and between things.

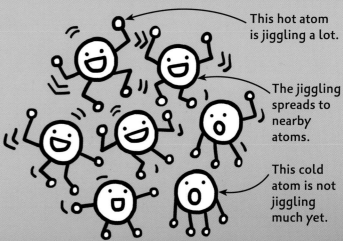

This hot atom is jiggling a lot.

The jiggling spreads to nearby atoms.

This cold atom is not jiggling much yet.

1 To prepare this trick, first fill two empty bottles with rice using a funnel.

2 Tap one of the bottles a few times on a hard surface. The rice will become more tightly packed and space will appear at the top of the bottle.

CHOPSTICK

Hidden forces are at work in this fun challenge. Ask a friend to pick up a bottle of rice with a chopstick. They won't be able to do it, but you will...

CHALLENGE

I'VE GOT THE POWER!

YOU WILL NEED
* Rice
* Funnel
* Two empty bottles
* Chopsticks

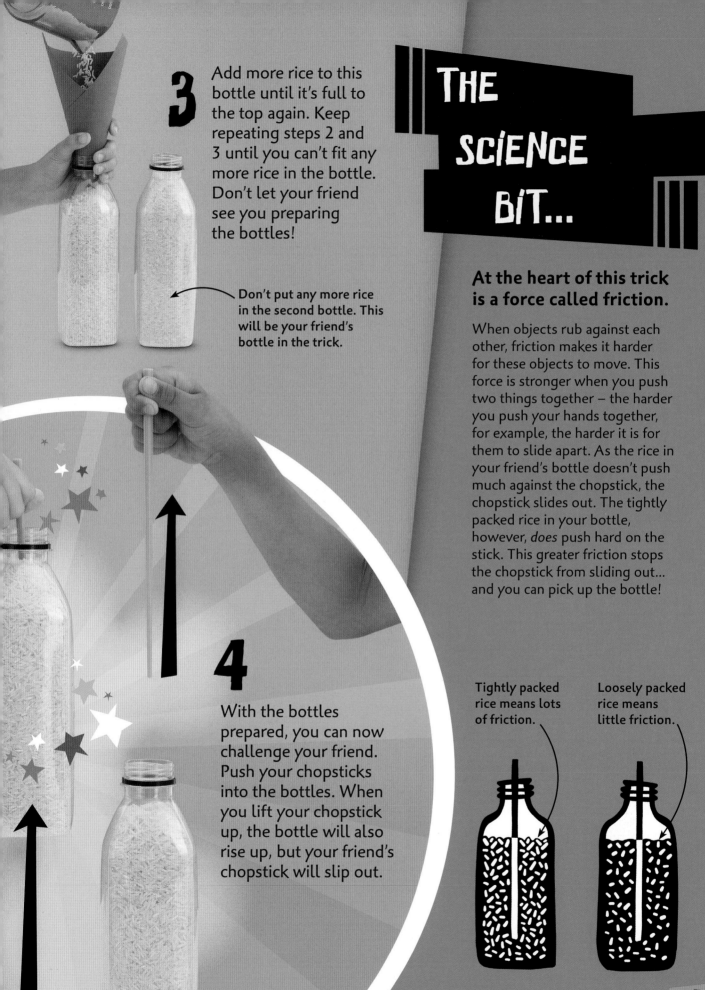

3 Add more rice to this bottle until it's full to the top again. Keep repeating steps 2 and 3 until you can't fit any more rice in the bottle. Don't let your friend see you preparing the bottles!

Don't put any more rice in the second bottle. This will be your friend's bottle in the trick.

4 With the bottles prepared, you can now challenge your friend. Push your chopsticks into the bottles. When you lift your chopstick up, the bottle will also rise up, but your friend's chopstick will slip out.

THE SCIENCE BIT...

At the heart of this trick is a force called friction.

When objects rub against each other, friction makes it harder for these objects to move. This force is stronger when you push two things together – the harder you push your hands together, for example, the harder it is for them to slide apart. As the rice in your friend's bottle doesn't push much against the chopstick, the chopstick slides out. The tightly packed rice in your bottle, however, *does* push hard on the stick. This greater friction stops the chopstick from sliding out... and you can pick up the bottle!

Tightly packed rice means lots of friction.

Loosely packed rice means little friction.

YOU WILL NEED
* Unopened bottle of spring water
* Bottle of tap water
* A freezer
* Ice cube

Keep an eye on the clock!

1

Put one unopened bottle of spring water and one tester bottle of tap water in the freezer. After 2 hours, check every 15 minutes until the tap water is frozen. Remove this from the freezer, or it may explode!

2

Remove the unopened spring water from the freezer. It should still be liquid, but supercooled below zero. Take care not to knock the bottle, it might instantly freeze! Open it and slowly pour the water over an ice cube.

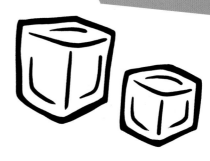

MAGIC ICE TOWER

You might know that water turns to ice at 0°C (32°F), but did you know that it can stay liquid below this temperature? Here's how to supercool water with magic results.

3 As the supercooled water touches the ice, it freezes. Keep pouring the water onto the ice cube – it will grow into a knobbly, twisty tower.

THE SCIENCE BIT...

Water freezes at zero... but only if it has somewhere to get started!

Water molecules join the ice crystal.

Ice crystal structure

In tap water, ice crystals form around tiny dust particles. That's why the tap water froze and the spring water – with no particles in it – stayed a liquid. Water also freezes on contact with ice, which explains why the supercooled spring water turns into ice instantly on the cube. When the water hits the ice, free-floating water molecules snap into position on an ice crystal and the tower grows.

1 Point the hairdryer upwards and turn it on. Hold the ping-pong ball in the stream of air and let it go.

YOU WILL NEED
* Hairdryer
* Ping-pong ball

LOOK! THE BALL LEVITATES!

FLOATING PING-PONG BALL

Levitation, or floating, is a skill all magicians should have. We can show you how to master it using the science of airflow.

THE SCIENCE BIT...

FORCE OF THE AIR

FORCE OF GRAVITY

The secret behind what's going on here is all to do with balancing forces.

Gravity – the force that pulls us towards the ground – pulls the ping-pong ball downwards, while the force of the hairdryer's stream of air pushes the ball upwards. When these forces are exactly balanced, the ball doesn't move up or down. You may wonder why the ball doesn't "fall off" when you tilt the hairdryer. This is down to something called the Coandă effect – when air moves over a surface, it will stick to that surface a little. So the air streaming past the ping-pong ball sticks to it and holds it in place.

2

Tilt the hairdryer a little to the side. Amazingly, the ball will stay in the stream of air and not drop down.

NOW TRY THIS

Here's another way of seeing the Coandă effect in action. Place a bottle in front of a paper windmill and blow directly at the bottle. The windmill will turn because the air from your breath sticks to the bottle and curves around it to move the sails. Cool, eh?

THE CHAIN FOUNTAIN

When a chain of beads is pulled from a pot, something amazing happens. The chain continues to pour out on its own and actually rises up into the air! It seems like magic but it's all about forces...

THE MOULD EFFECT

This works with the type of chain you find attached to a bath plug, only a lot longer. After the chain is carefully fed into a glass jar, the end is pulled out until it starts flowing on its own... with surprising results. It was discovered by the author of this book, which is why it's called the Mould effect.

CHAIN OF BEADS

Pull the end of the chain out and let it fall...

70

WORKING IT OUT

The chain fountain was a mystery until two scientists, John Biggins and Mark Warner, worked out what was going on. They showed that just as the chain leaves the pile, it pushes down a little on the pile. Thanks to Isaac Newton and his laws of motion, we know that when you push something, that thing pushes back. So the pile pushes back on the chain, causing it to rise up.

The chain pushes the pile down... and the pile pushes the chain up!

THE BEADS GO UP BEFORE THEY GO DOWN!

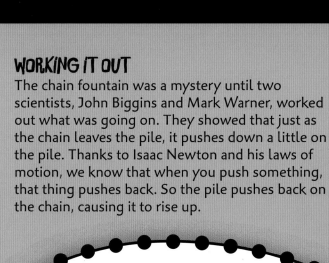

...then watch the beads fly!

GOING HIGHER

If you can make the chain fall faster, you increase the pushing forces and the chain rises even higher. To do this, you raise the jar higher so the chain has further to fall. The record is a 1.5 m (5 ft) high loop above the jar!

PUZZLING BOULDERS

These giant rocks are found all over Karlu Karlu in northern Australia. They balance on hilltops and some are even stacked on top of each other. How did they get to be in such strange locations?

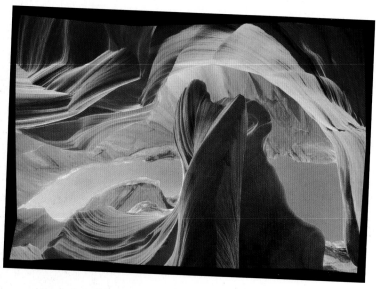

SHAPED BY NATURE

Rocks are worn down by water, wind, and the weather. This erosion is responsible for incredible formations all over the world, like the beautiful Antelope Canyon in Arizona, USA. Floodwaters slowly eroded the sandstone over millions of years to create these amazing colourful sculptures.

DEVIL'S MARBLES

The Karlu Karlu boulders are also known as the Devil's Marbles. You might wonder who, or what, had the strength to roll them into place. The truth is that they're all that's left from the erosion, or natural wearing away, of the rock and earth that surrounded them.

* Two forks
* Wooden toothpick
* A glass

1 Push two forks together as shown in this picture. Use enough force for the forks to stay in position, but be careful not to poke yourself.

Make sure the two forks are tightly connected.

2 Push a toothpick through a gap between the prongs of the forks.

Insert about a third of the toothpick through the gap.

BALANCING ACT

Challenge a friend to balance two forks over a glass using just a wooden toothpick. Impossible! Yet after we show you how, you'll be able to impress your buddies with these amazing balancing skills.

THE SCIENCE BIT...

The forks might seem like they are defying gravity, but it's all to do with something called the centre of mass.

This is the central point of the total weight of something. It is where everything is perfectly balanced. The diagram shows the centre of mass just below where the toothpick touches the glass. By resting the toothpick on the rim of the glass at exactly this point, the forks are able to balance.

Centre of mass

3 Place the toothpick on the rim of a glass. Carefully adjust the position of the toothpick until the forks balance. They should not be touching the floor.

THE FORKS LOOK LIKE THEY'RE FLOATING!

* Sheet of paper
* White wax crayon or candle
* Permanent marker (optional)
* Paintbrush
* Watercolour paint

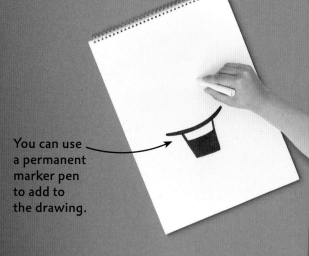

You can use a permanent marker pen to add to the drawing.

1 Draw a picture or write a message on white paper using the white crayon. It will be invisible.

2 Send or give the sheet of paper to your friend. To reveal the picture, they should start at the top of the paper and paint over it with watercolour paint.

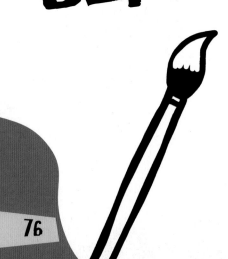

SEND A SECRET

If you've ever wanted to pull a rabbit out of a hat like a real magician, here's your chance. Once you learn this invisible ink trick, you will be able to send your friends any drawing or message... in secret.

THE SCIENCE BIT...

It's about how water and wax interact.

In a water-based paint like watercolour, tiny water particles are attracted to particles in the paper, so they soak into it. However, water particles are not attracted to wax particles. In fact, the water particles are more attracted to each other! So the water sticks together in droplets that roll off the wax. This is why the wax parts of the drawing do not absorb the paint and stay white.

Water droplets roll off the wax.

WATER ON WAX PAPER

Raincoats are made of materials that don't absorb water. Some have a wax coating.

RAINCOAT

WHAT'S THAT IN THE HAT?

IT'S A RABBIT!

3

Ta-da! The picture is revealed. The strange thing is that it's made up of all the bits where the paint *didn't* go!

DISAPPEARING STATUE OF LIBERTY

In 1983, illusionist David Copperfield carried out an unbelievable trick – he made the Statue of Liberty in New York City, USA, disappear. Here's how he fooled millions of amazed viewers.

WATCHING ON TV AND IN PERSON
The trick was billed as "The Illusion of the Century", with Copperfield saying that he would make the 93 m (305 ft) statue disappear before a live television audience of millions. To prove to TV viewers that this wasn't just camera trickery, a few spectators were invited to witness the stunt in person.

78

HOW THE ILLUSION UNFOLDED

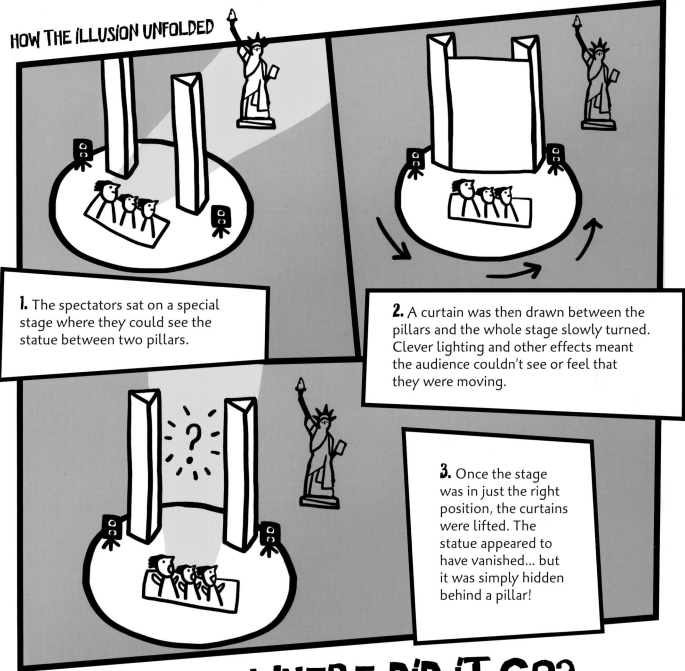

1. The spectators sat on a special stage where they could see the statue between two pillars.

2. A curtain was then drawn between the pillars and the whole stage slowly turned. Clever lighting and other effects meant the audience couldn't see or feel that they were moving.

3. Once the stage was in just the right position, the curtains were lifted. The statue appeared to have vanished... but it was simply hidden behind a pillar!

NO WAY! WHERE DID IT GO?

MAKING THE GROUND SHAKE

It's easy to tell when you're standing on a moving stage because you can feel a rumbling under your feet. To disguise this, Copperfield played loud music through large speakers. This made the floor rumble, which covered up the movement of the turning stage. By tricking their senses, the illusionist fooled spectators into believing the stunt was real.

GLOW IN THE DARK

Who needs a lamp when your body is a torch? Certainly not the firefly, which is one of a few incredible animals that uses bioluminescence – where a creature can make its own light – to glow in the dark.

TWINKLING IN THE TREES
This may look like a fairytale forest, but it's actually a throng of fireflies. These ones emit a yellow light, but other species glow green, blue, and pale red. Large groups can flash their lights on and off together with perfect timing. The flashes are used for defence, to communicate, and by males to attract females.

FABULOUS FIREFLIES

Fireflies are not actually flies, but a type of flying beetle. They have a special organ in their abdomen – the lower-rear part of their body – where chemicals are mixed together, including one that reacts with oxygen to produce light. By switching the supply of oxygen on and off, the firefly is able to control the speed and brightness of the flash.

Abdomen

BENDY WATER

Some magicians say they can move objects with the power of their mind. Here's how you can move water with the power of science.

YOU WILL NEED
* Paper cup
* Sharp pencil
* Inflated balloon
* Water

1 Turn a paper cup upside down and carefully make a hole in the bottom of it with a sharp pencil.

2 Rub the balloon on your hair. After rubbing for quite a long time, your hair should stick to the balloon!

3 Hold the cup over a sink or bowl and fill it with water. Watch it flow out of the hole in a thin stream.

The water will flow out in a straight line.

THE SCIENCE BIT...

Everything is made of tiny particles, and most of these particles have something called an "electric charge".

There are two types of charge – positive and negative. Positive particles are attracted to negative particles. To begin with, positive and negative particles in the balloon are perfectly balanced. But when you rub the balloon against your hair, some negatively charged particles called electrons transfer from your hair onto the balloon. Water molecules, groups of tiny particles, are positive at one end and negative at the other. The positive ends are attracted to the extra negative particles in the balloon, causing the stream of water to curve.

4

Move the balloon towards the stream of water and watch it magically bend!

RUBBING YOUR SHOES ON A CARPET WILL CHARGE UP YOUR BODY JUST LIKE THE BALLOON!

WATER MOLECULES   BALLOON

Positive end

Negative end

Negatively charged electrons

YOU WILL NEED

* Liquid latex
* Bowl
* Food dye (optional)
* Spoon
* Vinegar

1 Pour about two tablespoons of liquid latex into a bowl.

2 If you want a colourful ball, add some food dye to the bowl.

3 Add about two tablespoons of vinegar. Stir the mixture together in a gentle rolling motion for about one minute until it starts to set.

RUBBER BALL CAULDRON

Witches and wizards magically make things by mixing ingredients in a cauldron. Here we'll show you how to mix a potion to make a ball that will leave you bouncing with joy.

4 Remove the lump of mixture from the bowl. Then roll it between your hands until...

5 ...you've made your own bouncy rubber ball!

HOW FAR WILL IT **BOUNCE?**

THE SCIENCE BIT...

Ammonia stops rubber polymers sticking together.

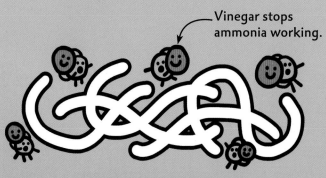

RUBBER POLYMERS SLIPPING AND SLIDING PAST EACH OTHER

Vinegar stops ammonia working.

RUBBER POLYMERS STICKING TOGETHER

Rubber is an example of a polymer, meaning it's made of really long chains of ball-like particles called atoms.

These polymer chains slip and slide around each other thanks to a chemical called ammonia, which stops them from sticking together. When you add vinegar to liquid rubber, it reacts with the ammonia and stops it from working. The polymers now stick together and form a solid mass – your rubber ball!

YOU WILL NEED
* Handful of same-sized coins
* Blindfold (or scarf)

Mystify your friends with money magic in this simple but impressive coin trick. The best bit? It's all down to some clever maths, so it works every time.

MATHEMATICAL COIN MAGIC

1 Ask a friend to shake at least eight coins in their hands, then lay the coins on the table.

2 Secretly count the number of coins that are facing heads up.

3 Put on a blindfold and tell your friend to rearrange the coins as much as they like, but without lifting them off the table. Say that you are now going to split the coins into two piles, both of which will have the same number of heads.

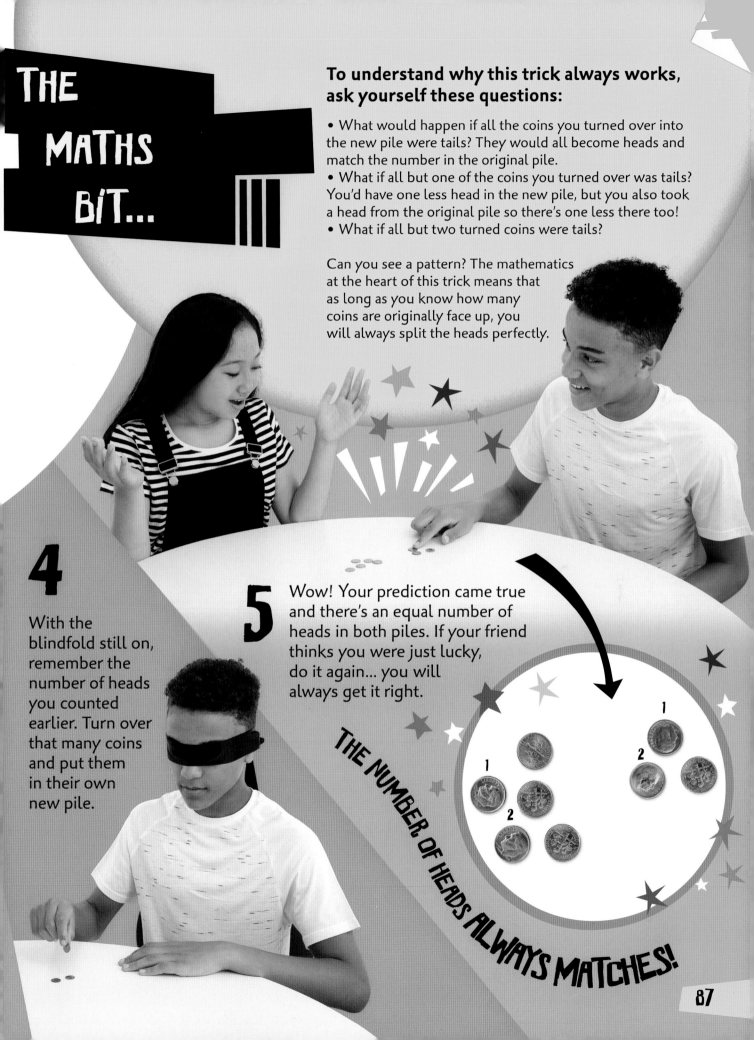

To understand why this trick always works, ask yourself these questions:

• What would happen if all the coins you turned over into the new pile were tails? They would all become heads and match the number in the original pile.

• What if all but one of the coins you turned over was tails? You'd have one less head in the new pile, but you also took a head from the original pile so there's one less there too!

• What if all but two turned coins were tails?

Can you see a pattern? The mathematics at the heart of this trick means that as long as you know how many coins are originally face up, you will always split the heads perfectly.

4

With the blindfold still on, remember the number of heads you counted earlier. Turn over that many coins and put them in their own new pile.

5 Wow! Your prediction came true and there's an equal number of heads in both piles. If your friend thinks you were just lucky, do it again... you will always get it right.

THE NUMBER OF HEADS ALWAYS MATCHES!

1
2
1
2

THE FLOATING PAPERCLIP

With this trick you will amaze your (mere mortal) friends by making a paperclip float.

YOU WILL NEED
* Two paperclips
* Glass of water

1 Give your friend two paperclips. Ask them to get at least one to float in a glass of water. They will sink every time!

DOWN IT GOES!

2 Take one of the paperclips and bend it into this shape.

3 Place the other paperclip flat on the first paper clip so it makes a cross shape.

You will have to balance this paperclip very carefully.

4 Using the first paperclip as a handle, slowly lower the second one onto the water. Keeping the second paperclip horizontal, push the first one down into the water and away from the now floating paperclip.

Try to keep your hand as steady as possible.

IT FLOATS!
IT REALLY FLOATS!

THE SCIENCE BIT...

The paperclip floats because of something called surface tension.

Water is made of tiny particles that stick to each other. Because those at the surface have nothing above them, their sticking power is stronger on the surface. This forms a tight, stretchy skin that is strong enough to support a – carefully positioned – paperclip.

Water particles stick together more strongly on the surface.

WALKING ON WATER
Some insects use surface tension to walk on water. Pond skaters have special pads on their feet covered in waxy, waterproof hairs. Their feet dent the surface, but the surface tension keeps them afloat.

BED of NAILS

First things first – lying on a bed of nails is only carried out by professionals. You should NEVER lay down on a nail! It's really dangerous. So you would think that laying on thousands of them would be thousands of times worse. Except it isn't...

A STAGE CLASSIC

Lying on a bed of nails is a traditional form of meditation practised by Indian holy men. However, for many years it has also been a popular stage act. In it, daring performers would risk having their bodies spiked by nails for the amusement of the audience. This brave entertainer is the filling in a nail sandwich.

A Thousand Nails are Better Than One

If you were to push a balloon onto a nail (**do not try this at home!**), you wouldn't need to push very hard before it popped. This is because all of your pushing force is concentrated on one nail. Yet pressed onto many nails, the balloon won't burst – the pushing force is shared across the nails and is not enough to pop the balloon. The same is true with nails and the skin on a human body.

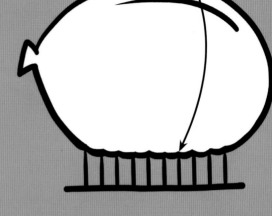

Force is spread over many points.

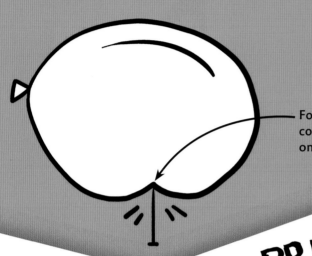

Force is concentrated on a tiny point.

IT'S ALL ABOUT PRESSURE!

PRESSURE POINTS

When force is concentrated on a small area, we say that the pressure is high. When it's spread out, we say it's low. The trick always uses blunt nails with a larger surface area than sharp nails, so pressure is low and the skin is not pierced.

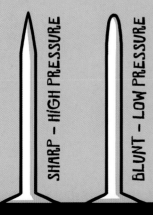

SHARP – HIGH PRESSURE

BLUNT – LOW PRESSURE

HIGH-HEEL SHOE

A high heel has a small area, so the pressure is high.

An elephant may be heavy, but its wide foot spreads the weight, so the pressure is low.

ELEPHANT FOOT

GLOSSARY

air pressure force of air that presses down on a surface

atmosphere layer of gases that surrounds a planet

atoms tiny particles. Atoms make up all matter

aurora bands of coloured light in the night sky, especially in polar regions

balance sense that stops a person from falling over; the even spread of the weight of an object, keeping it upright and steady

bioluminescence ability of some living things to produce and give off light

blind spot small area of the retina in the eye that is not sensitive to light. Nerve fibres leave the eye at the blind spot and form the optic nerve

chromatophore type of skin cell that contains a sac of coloured chemical. If the sac is stretched out, the cell changes colour

conductor substance that allows heat or electricity to pass through it easily

crystal solid with a recognizable shape, such as a cube

electron one of three types of tiny particle inside an atom. Electricity is the flow of electrons

erosion changes in the surface of the Earth as features get worn away by the weather

escapologist performer who escapes from restraints, such as hand cuffs, ropes, or chains, as quickly as possible

force push or pull that causes things to move, change direction, change speed, or stop moving

friction force that stops objects from sliding over each other

gravity force that pulls one object towards another. Gravity is the reason why objects fall to the ground

inertia tendency everything has to avoid movement or change

infrared type of light that feels warm but is invisible to humans

"Jastrow illusion" visual trick in which two identical curved shapes are placed together in a way that makes them look like they are different sizes

levitation act of rising or floating in the air

light spectrum range of light colours, from red to violet, that our eyes can detect

lung capacity total amount of air that someone can take into their lungs after breathing in very deeply

magnet piece of iron or other material that can attract another magnetic material

meditation practice of clearing or focusing the mind

oil liquid that does not mix with water

optic nerve bundle of nerves carrying electrical signals from the retina in the eye to the brain

photoreceptor type of cell in the retina of the eye that detects light

pixel tiny area on a display screen. Many pixels make up an image

polymer groups of atoms locked together in a long chain

retina light-sensitive lining at the back of the eye

sensor electronic device in a digital camera that uses light to form an

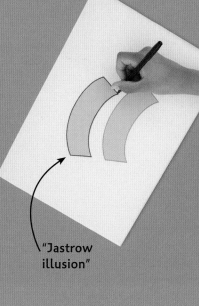

"Jastrow illusion"

image made up of pixels on the display screen

solar wind fast stream of particles flowing out of the Sun and across the Solar System

surface tension force caused by tiny water particles sticking to each other, forming a type of skin on the surface

tendon band of tough tissue that connects a muscle to a bone

INDEX

ACKNOWLEDGEMENTS

The publisher would like to thank the following people for their assistance in the preparation of this book: Jolyon Goddard and Sally Beets for editorial assistance; Seepiya Sahni for design assistance; Caroline Hunt for proofreading; Helen Peters for the index; Lol Johnson and Ruth Jenkinson for photography; Eddie, Jaiden, Jamie, Lola, Mariah, and Ryhanna for modelling; and Anne Damerell for legal assistance.

Steve Mould would like to dedicate this book to Mum and Dad.

WHAT PICTURES ARE HIDDEN ON PAGES 54-55?
Look hard and you will see stars (p54) and a horse (p55). If you use the same technique to look *through* the patterns on the inside front and inside back covers of this book, you might discover even more stars!

The publisher would like to thank the following for their kind permission to reproduce their photographs:

(Key: a-above; b-below/bottom; c-centre; f-far; l-left; r-right; t-top)

11 Alamy Stock Photo: EyeEm (br). **13 Dreamstime.com:** ForeverLee (bl). **14 Alamy Stock Photo:** Everett Collection Historical (bl). **Dorling Kindersley:** Davenport's Magic kingdom (cra). **15 Dreamstime.com:** Petrjoura (cr). **16-17 naturepl.com:** Nature Production. **17 Alamy Stock Photo:** Paulo Oliveira (tr). **21 Dreamstime.com:** Antonio Gravante (clb). **PunchStock:** Steve Smith (c). **28 Getty Images:** Steffen Schnur. **30 Dreamstime.com:** Saitharn Samathong (c, cl). **31 Alamy Stock Photo:** Cultura RM (br). **Dreamstime.com:** Alen Dobric (ca). **Science Photo Library:** Giphotostock (cr). **37 123RF.com:** Yurii Perepadia (br). **38 Bridgeman Images:** A. Ganot, Natural Philosphy, London, 1887. / Universal History Archive / UIG. **39 Alamy Stock Photo:** DonSmith (bl). **40-41 Alamy Stock Photo:** Paul Brady. **44 Dreamstime.com:** Sergey Dolgikh / Dolgikh (br). **50 Getty Images:**

DeAgostini. **51 Depositphotos Inc:** vareika_tamara (cr). **52 Alamy Stock Photo:** Rolf Nussbaumer Photography (clb). **52-53 Getty Images:** Wild Horizons / UIG. **53 Science Photo Library:** Pascal Goetgheluck (bc, br). **55 Alamy Stock Photo:** Panther Media GmbH (ca). **57 Dreamstime.com:** Kenzenbrv (bc). **60 Mary Evans Picture Library. 61 Alamy Stock Photo:** imageBROKER (bl). **72 Alamy Stock Photo:** Edwin Verin (clb). **72-73 Alamy Stock Photo:** Ingo Oeland. **77 Dreamstime.com:** Maxim Kostenko (cra). **78 Alamy Stock Photo:** Everett Collection Inc (bl). **80-81 Getty Images:** Kei Nomiyama / Barcroft Images / Barcroft Media. **81 naturepl.com:** John Abbott (t, t/Firefly). **89 123RF.com:** poonotsuke (crb). **90 Getty Images:** Jeff Goode / Toronto Star. **91 Dorling Kindersley:** Colchester Zoo (br). **Dreamstime.com:** Ljupco (cb).

All further images © Dorling Kindersley For further information see: www.dkimages.com